YOUR KNOWLEDGE HAS VALUE

- We will publish your bachelor's and
  master's thesis, essays and papers

- Your own eBook and book -
  sold worldwide in all relevant shops

- Earn money with each sale

Upload your text at www.GRIN.com
and publish for free

James Sunney Quaicoe

Equipping Educational Administrators and Supervisors at the Metro Education Office with skills in the use of computers

GRIN Verlag

Bibliografische Information der Deutschen Nationalbibliothek:

Die Deutsche Bibliothek verzeichnet diese Publikation in der Deutschen National-
bibliografie; detaillierte bibliografische Daten sind im Internet über http://dnb.d-
nb.de/ abrufbar.

Imprint:

Copyright © 2011 GRIN Verlag GmbH
Druck und Bindung: Books on Demand GmbH, Norderstedt Germany
ISBN: 978-3-656-34554-1

This book at GRIN:

http://www.grin.com/en/e-book/202586/equipping-educational-administrators-and-
supervisors-at-the-metro-education

GRIN - Your knowledge has value

Der GRIN Verlag publiziert seit 1998 wissenschaftliche Arbeiten von Studenten, Hochschullehrern und anderen Akademikern als eBook und gedrucktes Buch. Die Verlagswebsite www.grin.com ist die ideale Plattform zur Veröffentlichung von Hausarbeiten, Abschlussarbeiten, wissenschaftlichen Aufsätzen, Dissertationen und Fachbüchern.

Visit us on the internet:

http://www.grin.com/

http://www.facebook.com/grincom

http://www.twitter.com/grin_com

UNIVERSITY OF CAPE COAST

CENTRE FOR CONTINUING EDUCATION

COURSE

EIT 505 Instructional design and development

TITLE:

Equipping Educational Administrators and Supervisors

at the Metro Education Office with skills in the use of computers

WRITTEN BY:

James Sunney Quaicoe

1

INTRODUCTION

The impact of technology on the educational systems across nations is enormous. Dlodlo and Sithole (2001), acknowledged that ICT is the fastest growing technology in this dispensation and that its influence pervade all spheres of human performance. Man's activities have become more knowledge driven – using emerging Information Communication Technologies (ICTs) such as computers, internet, digital equipment, mobile phones, chat engines and many other digital and multimedia communication technologies as the driving force in this direction.

In a practical illustration, Molosi (2001) observed that the internet used only four years to reach fifty million users, while Television took thirteen years to attain the same number of viewers. This goes to illustrate the speed at which technology is advancing. This trend has brought to the fore the need for integration of ICT in the education. Ghana in her 2007 New Education Reform (NER) made ICT a subject to be taught in school for the first time and became examinable in Basic Education Certificate Examination (BECE).

The success of the study of ICT in schools is linked the ability of Educational Administrators and Supervisors offer the technology based leadership. Consequently, supports Supervisors and Educational Administrators need to be equip with some level of ICT stills in order undertake any effective   monitoring,. In effect, , if Educational administrators or supervisors lack the basic knowledge on ICTs or computers they may not be effective in accomplishing their duties.

In the light of the above, it has become expedient for the Educational Administrators and Circuit Supervisors at the Metro Education Office, Takoradi in Ghana to be equipped with skills in the use Computers and their associated basic applications.

PERFORMANCE ANALYSIS

To obtain the source of the problem pertaining to this assessment, a questionnaire was used to obtain the demographic information, level of education, knowledge in computers, knowledge on applications software and experience in the job, among other things pertaining to ICT/Computer use.

Methodology:

A questionnaire with a four-point Likert scale was design to establish the ICT and Computer application knowledge skills level of Educational Administrators and Circuit Supervisors in the following areas ; Basic Computer Operations, File Management, Word Processing, Spreadsheet Use, Database Use, and Internet Use. In addition, the instrument contained a part that offered the target population to provide their demographic data.

Target Population Analysis:

Educational Administrators and Circuit Supervisor – constituted the target population and they were thirty (30) in number. The break down was nine (9) males and twenty-one (21) females. The average age of the staff members is 40 years with the youngest having an age of twenty-eight (28) years and the eldest being forty-five (45) years old.

Education/Qualification:

A total of forty (40) percent of the have Teachers' Certificate A – out of the percentage ninety -five (95) percent hold either a first degree or diploma certificate. Five percent are holding second degrees.

Language:

In addition to the English Language – which is the official Language, each of the officers could also speak the local language predominantly used in the Sekondi Takoradi area.

ICT Knowledge:

1. Some Staff members have average computer literacy skills.

2. Not all have had basic instruction in computer use.

3. Most of the officers are not active users of computers.

Work Experience:

The target population have average work experiences of twelve (12) years. Each of them had taught in the classroom for not less than four (4) years.

Motivation:

Most staff members see it as exciting that if their technology knowledge could be enhanced through a practical capacity building activity.

GOAL ANALYSIS RESULTS

General goals:

Educational officers will be able to undertake basic computer operations using selected MS Suite Applications.

Specific Goals:

The capacity building activity for the officers would cover the under listed areas :

1. Basic computer operations
2. Creation of folders
3. Creation of word document
4. Creation of simple worksheet
5. Creation of simple presentation
6. Creation of simple database
7. Saving created work
8. Cutting and pasting of work
9. Copying and pasting of work
10. Using of the internet

Refining/Refined Goals:

1. Create a word document
2. Create a simple worksheet
3. Create a simple presentation
4. Create a simple database
5. Copy and paste a work
6. Use the internet

7. Undertake basic computer operations

8. Create a folder

9. Cut and paste work

10. Save a work

Ranking/Ranked goals:

1. Use the internet

2. Undertake basic computer operations

3. Create a folder

4. Cut and paste work

5. Save a work

6. Create a word document

7. Create a simple worksheet

8. Create a simple presentation

9. Create a simple database

10. Copy and paste a work

Refine goals again:

1. Undertake basic computer operations

2. Save a work

3. Editing work

4. Create a word document

5. Create a simple worksheet

6. Create a simple presentation

7. Create a simple database

8. Cut and paste a work

Final ranking:

1. Undertake basic computer operations
2. Create a word document
3. Editing work
4. Use the internet
5. Create a simple worksheet
6. Create a simple presentation
7. Create a simple database

Learning Objectives:

By the end of the capacity development exercise, learners should be able to;

a. Undertake basic computer operations
b. Create a word document
c. Create a folder
d. Save a document
e. Copy and paste a work
f. Cut and paste a work
g. Use the internet
h. Create a simple worksheet
i. Create a simple presentation
j. Create a simple database

TASK ANALYSIS

Task 1: Undertake basic computer operations.

Sub task

1. Basic computer operations facts;

   – Learners memorise the facts about basic computer operations, including names of parts, applications and their specific functions.

2. Basic computer operations procedure;

   - Learners to follow ordered steps to boot computers, shut down computers and launch an application.

3. Basic computer operations principles and rules;

   - Learners to observe the rules of booting and shutting down computers.

4. Basic computer operations attitudes;

   - Learners to develop right attitudes to computer use - by way of observing computer use ethics.

Task 2: Create a word document

Sub task

1. Facts

   - Learners identify the functional applications and parts of word-processing applications.

2. Procedure

   - Learners follow the sequence of launching MS Word Applications

   - Follow procedures to pull down or open menus and commands.

8

3. Principles and rules

 - Learners to internalize the principle of making a document private or
   public.

Task 3: Create a folder

Sub task

1. Facts

 - Learners indentify the facts associated with file / folder creation and the
   various components and commands facilitating the task.

2. Procedure

 - Learners follow sequential steps to create a folder.

3 Attitudes

 - Learners adhere to safety in documents in the context of being confidential
   (restricted access) or shares publicly.

Task 4: Save a document

Sub task

1. Facts

 - Learners identify the facts associated with saving a document, such as save
   command and save as command.

2. Procedure

 - Learners to follow the procedure for saving new files and edited
   documents.

3. Principles and rules

 - Learners to learn the rules that unsaved files or documents would be lost.

4. Attitudes

   - Learners to exhibit caution in safe keeping of documents to avoid losing
     them.

Task 5: Copy and paste a work

Sub task

1. Facts

   - Learners to identify the facts linked to the copy and paste tasks in
     computing.

2. Procedure

   - Procedures are to be followed by learners to copy text, picture or graphics
     from one point to another on a document.

3. Principles and rules

   - Learners to learn the rule that material   to be copied are selected.

Task 6: Cut and paste a work

Sub task

1. Facts

   - Learners to identify the facts linked to the cut and paste tasks in
     computing.

2. Procedure

   - Procedures are to be followed by learners to copy text, picture or graphics
     from one point to another on a document.

3. Principles and rules

-   Procedures are to be followed by learners to cut text, picture or graphics from one point to another on a document.

4. Attitudes

-   Learners adhere to safety in documents storage to avoid lost of files.

Task 7: Use the internet

Sub task

1. Facts

-   Learners identify facts surrounding the internet use, the functions of the search engines and the emails.

2. Procedure

-   Learners follow the various procedures to launch the internet, locate a service provider and use search engines for information search.

3. Principles and rules

-   Learners to adhere to netiquette requirements

4. Attitudes

-   Learners to be particular about hazardous software and harmful sites.

Task 8: Create a simple worksheet

Sub task

1   Facts

-   Learners identify the functional applications and parts of spread sheet applications.

2   Procedure

-   Learners follow the sequence of launching MS Excel Applications

- Follow procedures to pull down or open menus and commands.

3 Principles and rules

   - Learners to internalize the principle of making a document private or public.

4 Attitudes

   - Learners adhere to safety in documents storage to avoid lost of files.

Task 9: Create a simple presentation

Sub task

1 Facts

   - Learners identify the functional applications and parts of Presentation applications.

2 Procedure

   - Learners follow the sequence of launching MS PowerPoint Applications
   - Follow procedures to pull down or open menus and commands.

3 Principles and rules

   - Learners to internalize the principle of making a document private or public.

4 Attitudes

   - Learners adhere to safety in documents storage to avoid lost of files.

Task 10: Create a simple database

Sub task

1 Facts

- Learners identify the functional applications and parts of database applications.

2 Procedure

- Learners follow the sequence of launching MS Word Access
- Follow procedures to pull down or open menus and commands and launch applications

3 Principles and rules

- Learners to internalize the principle of making a document private or public.

4 Attitudes

- Learners adhere to safety in documents storage to avoid lost of files.

STRATEGY AND MEDIA ANALYSIS MATRIX

Topic/Sub-topic	Learning objective	Learning Task	Instructional Strategy	Media used
1. Undertake basic computer operations	Learners will be able to : - Boot a computer - Identify the parts and commands for booting and shutting down - Identify precautions to take	- Facts - Procedure - Principles and Rules - Attitude	Discussions, Demonstrations and Practise	Print, Text, Learning Packages and Computers
2. Create a word document	Learners will be able to : - Launch MS Word Applications - Indentify the parts and commands associated with undertaking word processing task. - Create a simple word document	- Facts - Procedure - Principles and Rules	Discussions, Demonstrations and Practise	Print, Text, Learning Packages and Computers
3. Create a folder	Learners will be able to : - Identify parts and commands for creating folders - Follow given procedure to create folder - Learners describe safety precautions to follow	- Facts - Procedure - Attitude	Discussions, Demonstrations and Practise	Print, Text, Learning Packages and Computers
4. Save a document	Learners will be able to : - Identify and locate positions of parts and commands for saving document. - Follow sequential steps to save a created document. - Describe safety precautions to adhere to.	- Facts - Procedure - Principles and Rules - Attitude	Discussions, Demonstrations and Practise	Print, Text, Learning Packages and Computers
5. Copy and paste a work	Learners will be able to : - Identify parts and commands for copying and pasting. - Follow outlined steps to copy and paste texts and graphics.	- Facts - Procedure - Principles and Rules	Discussions, Demonstrations and Practise	Print, Text, Learning Packages and Computers
6. Cut and paste a work	Learners will be able to : - Identify parts and commands for cutting and saving text and graphics. - Follow procedures to	- Facts - Procedure - Principles and Rules - Attitude	Discussions, Demonstrations and Practise	Print, Text, Learning Packages and Computers

	cut and paste text or graphics. - Describe safety precautions to avoid data loss.			
7. Use the internet	Learners will be able to : - Launch the internet browsers - Indentify the parts and commands for emailing and research work - Create a simple mail and search for information - Adhere to netiquettes and safety practices	- Facts - Procedure - Principles and Rules - Attitude	Discussions, Demonstrations and Practise	Print, Text, Learning Packages and Computers
8. Create a simple worksheet	Learners will be able to : - Launch MS Excel Applications - Indentify the parts and commands associated with undertaking spreadsheet task. - Create a simple spreadsheet document	- Facts - Procedure - Principles and Rules	Discussions, Demonstrations and Practise	Print, Text, Learning Packages and Computers
9. Create a simple presentation	Learners will be able to : - Launch MS PowerPoint Applications - Indentify the parts and commands associated with undertaking presentation task. - Create a simple presentation	- Facts - Procedure - Principles and Rules	Discussions, Demonstrations and Practise	Print, Text, Learning Packages and Computers
10. Create a simple database	Learners will be able to : - Launch Applications - Indentify the parts and commands processing a database task. - Create a simple database	- Facts - Procedure - Principles and Rules	Discussions, Demonstrations and Practise	Print, Text, Learning Packages and Computers

COST ANALYSIS

The cost analysis covered the design, implementation, evaluation and reporting of the needs assessment activity. It further looks at expenses for the actual training taking cognisance of the human and material resources required. Due to the fact that the contends of the training was loaded and also practical based, there was the need to camp the officers and take care of their meals so as to maximise the instructional time with the three days set for the training.

ITEM No.	NAMES/DESCRIPTION	QUANTITY	TOTAL COST (GHC)
1	Training - Planning, Implementation and Evaluation.		91.30
2	Computers and accessories	30	1500.00
3	Learning Packages	10	500.00
4	Training -materials		500.00
5	Instructors/Coaches	5	1000.00
6	Administrative Support		50.00
7	Projector	1	1300.00
8	Accommodation for Learners		1800.00
9	Learners' Meals	30	500.00
10	T & T for Learners	30	300.00
11	Instructors/Coaches T & T	5	300.00
12	Instructors/Coaches Meals	5	200.00
13	Instructors/Coaches Accommodation	5	500.00
14	Miscellaneous		200.00
TOTAL ESTIMATED EXPENDITURE			**7961.30**

REFERENCES

Dlodlo, N. & Sithole, N. 2001. The Internet as a tool for a revolution in education in Africa: A dream or reality. In C. Crawford et al. (Eds.), Proceedings of Society for Information Technology and Teacher Education International Conference 2001 (pp. 3038-3043). Chesapeake,VA: AACE .Retrived from http://news.educa.ch/de/literaturliste on April 7, 2010.

Molosi, K. (2001). Making the Internet work for Africa. *Computers in Africa, Oct./Nov., 37-38*

REFERENCES

Forte ... & ... , F. 2007. The history of ... applications ... ...
... ... In: ... ... (eds.), Data ... in ...
... for Information Technology and Social Change Management.
... ... , pp. 3628-3631. Conceptual ... ... , ... from
... .

... 2010.